Lovin Le the Way

Written by: Krystal Willoughby

Illustrated by: Katarzyna Kozakiewicz

ISBN:
978-1-63308-633-3 (paperback)
978-1-63308-634-0 (ebook)

Cover and Interior Design by *R'tor John D. Maghuyop*
Illustrated by *Katarzyna Kozakiewicz*

CHALFANT ECKERT
PUBLISHING

1028 S Bishop Avenue, Dept. 178
Rolla, MO 65401

Printed in United States of America

Lowin Leads the Way

Written by:
Krystal Willoughby

Illustrated by:
Katarzyna Kozakiewicz

Thank you...

2020 has been by far the hardest year of our lives so far, but it has also put so much into perspective. Our family has recieved so much giving, so much love, so much kindess. I havent been able to recognize everyone or individually thank ALOT of people, but please know Jake and I are forever grateful. We appreciate every single message recieved, every card, every gift to raise her spirits, every prayer chain we have been added to, every fundraiser in her name, every text, and call. As well as all the help and love poured into the boys. This list goes on and on and I could never put into words the amount of thanks and gratitude that fills our hearts. This year has reminded us of our dependence upon other people and how willing others are to step up and help.

A huge thanks and gratitude to the doctors, nurses, child life, therapists that have been with us from the beginning. We are so fortunate to live near a top rated hospital and get the best care for our girl!

Thank You Jesus, for not giving up on this weary mama. Thank You for reaching into my messy days. Thank you for grace in navigating this new world. Thank you for being our peace and light when the world feels dark and lonely. Thank you for the Christ-centered friendships that have become the branches that have softened the blow. Thank you for providing for and protecting us along the way.

My journey started just like
any regular day

But a big scary diagnosis got in the way

Hold on tight there will be
lots of stops

Some low valleys and others
high mountain tops

Some days
feel as dark
as night

But morning
always comes
with fresh
new light

Some will tell you
it can't be done

But I am a warrior and
I have just begun

My smile is always shining bright

Because Cancer did not know
I'd put up such a fight

I'm fierce, I'm strong, I'm brave, you see

Cancer picked the wrong kid when
it messed with me

Come with me friend,
take my hand

We can figure out together
what is planned

Making friends along
the way

Is what gets me through
each and every day

Made in the USA
Monee, IL
30 March 2021